7338 2615

1ST
IN FASHION
x x x x x

LEVI STRAUSS
BLUE JEAN GENIUS

ELSIE OLSON

Checkerboard Library

An Imprint of Abdo Publishing
abdopublishing.com

ABDOPUBLISHING.COM

Published by Abdo Publishing, a division of ABDO, PO Box 398166, Minneapolis, Minnesota 55439.
Copyright © 2018 by Abdo Consulting Group, Inc. International copyrights reserved in all countries.
No part of this book may be reproduced in any form without written permission from the publisher.
Checkerboard Library™ is a trademark and logo of Abdo Publishing.

Printed in the United States of America, North Mankato, Minnesota
062017
092017

Design: Emily O'Malley, Mighty Media, Inc.
Production: Emily O'Malley, Mighty Media, Inc.
Series Editor: Katherine Hengel Frankowski
Cover Photographs: Mighty Media, Inc. (right); Wikimedia Commons (left)
Interior Photographs: Alamy, p. 25; AP Images, p. 8 (middle); iStockphoto, pp. 5, 8 (bottom); Public domain, p. 17; Shutterstock, pp. 8 (top), 9 (top), 9 (middle), 9 (bottom), 19, 27; Wikimedia Commons, pp. 7, 11, 13, 15, 21, 23

Publisher's Cataloging-in-Publication Data

Names: Olson, Elsie, author.
Title: Levi Strauss: blue jean genius / by Elsie Olson.
Other titles: Blue jean genius
Description: Minneapolis, MN : Abdo Publishing, 2018. | Series: First in fashion |
    Includes bibliographical references and index.
Identifiers: LCCN 2016962493 | ISBN 9781532110771 (lib. bdg.) |
    ISBN 9781680788624 (ebook)
Subjects: LCSH: Strauss, Levi, 1829-1902--Juvenile literature. | Clothing trade--
    United States--Biography--Juvenile literature. | Jeans (Clothing)--United
    States--Biography--Juvenile literature.
Classification: DDC 746.9 [B]--dc23
LC record available at http://lccn.loc.gov/2016962493

CONTENTS

BLUE JEAN DREAMS

It's Friday morning, and you have a busy day ahead. First you have school, then you have to rake the yard. Finally, you have plans to go see a movie with some friends. What's the perfect fashion item for school, chores, and hanging out with friends? Blue jeans, of course!

Blue jeans are not only **versatile**. They're also sturdy. Most blue jeans are made from a strong fabric called **denim**. The pockets and seams on blue jeans are tough too. They are often secured using copper **rivets**, which reduce tearing.

Businessman Levi Strauss is considered the father of blue jeans. He popularized them in the 1870s. The pants Strauss helped to

FASHION FACTOID

The tiny pocket in the front of blue jeans was originally designed to hold a watch. This tiny pocket was a part of Levi Strauss's original pair of jeans.

Jeans come in many different shades and designs, so you can show off your own style!

create were first made popular by California gold miners. It didn't take long for them to be worn by ranchers, cowboys, and other workers too.

Today, blue jeans are worn by men, women, and children around the world. They've also become an important symbol of American **culture**. But blue jeans haven't always been so popular. In fact, there was a time when most people didn't wear pants at all!

PANTS OF THE PAST

Pants have been around for thousands of years. The oldest known pants were discovered in China. They were made of wool and are more than 3,000 years old!

Most people didn't wear pants in ancient times, though. Instead, most men and boys wore robes, **kilts**, or **tunics**. Women and girls typically wore robes or dresses. Pants were most often worn by people who rode horses. Wearing pants while riding was more comfortable than wearing a robe.

In the **Middle Ages**, many European men wore tunics and tights. By the 1600s, it was more fashionable for men to wear short pants called breeches. However, most farmers, sailors, and other laborers preferred the warmth and protection of long pants.

By the 1800s, long pants were popular workwear for men around the world. These pants were made from sturdy fabric and often dyed blue to hide work stains. In 1873, Levi Strauss helped make work pants even stronger. In time, his pants would become one of the most popular fashion items in the world.

It wasn't considered acceptable for women to wear pants until the early 1900s. Even then, women only wore pants for sports activities, such as bicycling.

FASHION
TIME MACHINE

LEVI STRAUSS & CO. XX, 1873 In the late 1800s, Levi Strauss & Co. released its XX work pants with copper **rivets** on the pockets and seams. The rivets helped support these areas, making the pants sturdier.

WOMEN'S JEANS, 1934 Levi Strauss & Co. released the first jeans designed for women in 1934. Before then, many women wore their husbands' jeans. Later styles were designed for fashion rather than **utility**.

FLARE JEANS, 1960s In the late 1960s, jeans that flared out at the ankles became popular. Nicknamed "bell-bottoms," these pants remained fashionable into the 1970s and made a comeback in the 1990s.

DISTRESSED JEANS, 1980s Punk rock musicians made ripped jeans popular. Young people started ripping their jeans to look like them. Soon, companies started distressing jeans to make them look worn.

BAGGY JEANS, 1990s Wide-leg jeans became popular in the 1990s. Many hip-hop artists, skateboarders, and punk musicians wore this style. A company named JNCO made a pair of very popular, superwide leg jeans.

SKINNY JEANS, 2000s Model Kate Moss began wearing skinny jeans in the early 2000s. These jeans were tight-fitting down to the ankles. Skateboarders and bike riders quickly adopted skinny jeans too.

THE BIRTH OF AN ICON

Loeb Strauss was born on February 26, 1829, in Buttenheim, Germany. His parents were Hirsch and Rebecca Strauss. Loeb was the youngest of seven children. He had one older sister and five older half siblings from his father's previous marriage.

The Strauss family practiced **Judaism**, which often made their lives challenging. For centuries, Jewish people have faced **discrimination** across the world. Germany in the 1800s was no exception. The Strauss family's hardships increased when Loeb's father died from **tuberculosis**. Following his death, the Strauss family decided it was time for a change.

Two of Loeb's brothers were living in the United States. Their names were Jonas and Louis. They lived in New York City. In 1846, Loeb, his mother, and two of his sisters joined them.

The house where Strauss and his family lived in Buttenheim, Germany, is now a historical monument and museum.

In New York City, Jonas and Louis ran a dry goods business. They sold fabric, clothing, bedding, and other nonfood items. The store was called J. Strauss Brother & Co. Loeb went to work for his brothers. He learned how to run a business. Around this time, Loeb's customers and family began calling him Levi.

GOLD!

As Levi adjusted to life in New York, the rest of the country was changing. In 1848, gold was discovered in California at Sutter's Mill. Between 1848 and 1852, more than 300,000 people flocked to California, seeking their fortunes. This movement of people became known as the Gold Rush.

The Gold Rush caused California's population to nearly double. To serve its growing citizenry, California needed more restaurants, hotels, and stores. Many businesspeople recognized the opportunity. Like the gold seekers, they made their way to California too.

The Strauss brothers knew California's new residents needed dry goods. So, they decided to open a **supply house** there. Levi would run this new operation. So, in 1853, Levi began his long journey to San Francisco, California. He was 24 years old.

The Gold Rush helped California become a US state. It became the thirty-first state on September 9, 1850.

In February 1853, Levi left New York City. He sailed to Panama, a small country that links Central and South America. He traveled west across Panama, and then boarded another ship that sailed north on the Pacific Ocean. He arrived in San Francisco on March 14, 1853.

SETTING UP SHOP

Soon after Strauss arrived in San Francisco, he opened his family's new **supply house** on Sacramento Street. It was close to the city's port, which made receiving shipped goods convenient. Strauss named the new business Levi Strauss.

Levi Strauss sold dry goods such as fabric, clothing, underwear, and umbrellas to small stores throughout the American West. These smaller stores would then sell the goods directly to customers. Because dry goods were in demand, Strauss could charge high prices. His supply house grew very quickly.

Throughout the 1850s, Strauss relocated his supply house to larger buildings several times. In 1863, he renamed his company Levi Strauss & Co. Three years later, he settled in a large space on Battery Street in San Francisco. This is where the company remained for the next 40 years.

The success of Strauss's company made him a well-known businessman. People in San Francisco and beyond knew his name. In 1872, a tailor from Reno, Nevada, sent Strauss a letter. The tailor's name was Jacob Davis, and the letter proposed an **intriguing** new partnership.

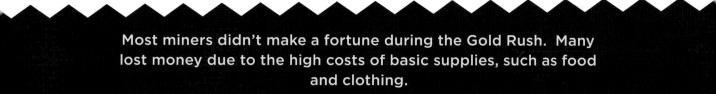

Most miners didn't make a fortune during the Gold Rush. Many lost money due to the high costs of basic supplies, such as food and clothing.

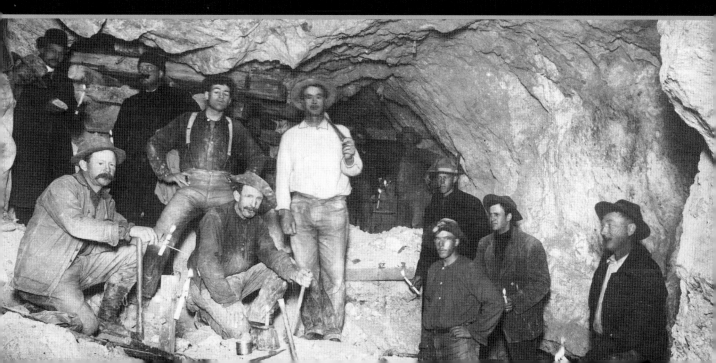

PANTS THAT LAST

∿∿∿

Davis was a regular Strauss customer. He used Strauss fabric to make goods for miners and other workers. In 1870, a woodcutter's wife came to Davis with a request. She asked him to make the strongest pair of pants for her husband that he could.

Davis used a sturdy cloth called duck cloth for the work pants. At the time, such types of work pants were known as *waist overalls* or *overalls*. Davis used copper **rivets** on the pockets and seams. The rivets helped prevent tears.

Davis sold the pants to the woodcutter's wife for $3.00. At the time, this was a high price. But she felt the quality was worth it. Soon, many of Davis's customers were asking for these special, sturdy work pants.

It was clear that Davis had created a **marketable** pair of pants. But he could not afford the fee to file a patent for them. So, he wrote to Strauss and suggested they work together. They'd apply for the patent together

Like Strauss, Davis was an immigrant. He moved from what is now Latvia to the United States in 1854.

and split the costs. Then Strauss could manufacture the pants. Strauss agreed, as long as Davis moved to San Francisco to oversee manufacturing. The men were awarded the patent on May 20, 1873.

MAKING LEVI'S

Strauss and Davis decided to make their pants using **denim**. This was more comfortable than duck cloth but just as sturdy. And, when dyed blue, denim could hide most work stains.

To make the pants, Levi Strauss & Co. delivered precut denim pieces to the homes of local **seamstresses**. They sewed the pants together and added the **rivets**. Then Levi Strauss & Co. sold the pants.

Strauss and Davis named their pants XX. This term was often used in the garment industry to indicate quality. But customers soon started calling the pants Levi's. The pants were so popular, the seamstresses couldn't make them fast enough! In the 1880s, Strauss and Davis opened their own factory. This allowed them to produce the pants more **efficiently**.

As Levi's popularity increased, other companies started making similar pants too. Strauss wanted to make sure

Not everyone in the United States could speak English or read. But the Levi's patch was so memorable, customers could still find the jeans they were looking for!

his pants were recognizable. So, in 1886, he added a leather patch to each pair. The patch soon became an iconic element of the Levi Strauss & Co. brand.

NEXT STEPS

In 1890, Davis and Strauss's patent ran out. Other companies could now legally imitate Levi's. But Strauss's work pants were one of the top-selling workwear pants. So, even without patent protection, Levi's continued to sell.

The same year, Levi's pants got a new name. They became known by their **lot numbers**. Strauss gave his popular XX Levi's the lot number 501. A less expensive version of the pants was given the lot number 201.

The company underwent other changes too. In the 1880s, Strauss had made four of his nephews part owners. Together, they **incorporated** the company in 1890. The company also started making more than just work pants. It began selling **denim** jackets and printed shirts too.

No matter the garment, Strauss clothing had a reputation for quality. Strauss had earned a positive

Philanthropy was very important to Strauss. He gave money to many charities.

reputation as a person too. He was a respected businessman, **philanthropist**, and San Francisco leader.

Strauss died at the age of 73 on September 26, 1902. He left his estate to his family and charities. After Strauss's death, his nephews took over running the business. Davis continued to oversee manufacturing for Levi Strauss & Co. until his death in 1908.

CHALLENGES & CHANGES

Four years after Strauss's death, his nephews faced an **incredible** challenge. In 1906, an extremely powerful earthquake shook the city of San Francisco. It killed 3,000 people and destroyed thousands of homes and businesses. Levi Strauss & Co. was among the companies destroyed.

After the earthquake, the Levi Strauss & Co. headquarters and factory had to be rebuilt. Strauss's nephews rallied together to save the business. Together, they successfully rebuilt everything from the ground up. Even after the earthquake, Levi Strauss & Co. remained as popular as ever.

ZIP IT UP

In the mid-1900s, Levi Strauss & Co. made a major change to its pants. It added a zipper! The original Levi's design used a button closure. But company leaders felt women would prefer zippers.

Levi's 501 jeans remained the best-selling workwear pants in the early 1900s. But they were only popular among men who worked outdoors. This changed in 1934 when Levi Strauss & Co. released its first pair of pants for women. These new pants were designed to be worn by women who were visiting ranches.

The 1906 earthquake remains the deadliest natural disaster in California history.

HELP FROM HOLLYWOOD

〰〰〰

Movies helped bring men's work pants into **mainstream** life. In 1955, the movie *Rebel Without a Cause* was released. The film starred actor James Dean. In it, Dean's character wears blue **denim** pants, a white T-shirt, and a leather jacket.

Many people who saw the movie admired Dean's character. They wanted to look like him. Blue denim pants became fashionable. More American men began wearing them, whether they were working or not.

The 1950s and 1960s brought other changes for denim pants. People began calling them jeans. In 1960, Levi Strauss & Co. replaced *overalls* with *jeans* on all its branding. Then, in 1961, another movie helped make

LOOK FOR THE TAB

In 1936, Levi Strauss & Co. added a small red tab to the right back pocket of its jeans. The tab is still on Levi's jeans today!

James Dean's style in *Rebel Without a Cause* is still one of the most iconic looks in film history.

women's jeans popular. That year, actor Marilyn Monroe starred in *The Misfits*. In the film, Monroe plays a woman who runs off with a group of cowboys. She wears jeans throughout the film. Women around the country started wearing jeans for fashion as well.

THE FUTURE OF LEVI'S

In 1959, Levi Strauss & Co. began exporting jeans to Europe. In 1965, the company set up divisions in Europe and Asia. By 1971, Levi's jeans were sold in 50 different countries. Jeans had officially become popular worldwide.

Today, Levi Strauss & Co. employs more than 12,500 people around the world. The company makes more than $4 billion per year. Its headquarters are still in San Francisco. And, Strauss's descendants still own the company.

Over the years, Levi Strauss & Co.'s product line has changed. Today, the company sells dress pants, dresses, skirts, shirts, and more. But it's still best-known for its jeans. The 501 remains one of the company's best-selling products.

Levi's jeans are now manufactured in many different styles, including flared, distressed, skinny, and more. The

Levi Strauss & Co. products are sold in 50,000 retail locations in more than 110 countries!

company also produces jeans made from stretchy **denim** to meet new customer tastes. Levi's jeans now come in many different shades of denim too.

Today, hundreds of companies manufacture and sell jeans. But Levi Strauss & Co. has remained one of the most popular jean brands in the world. After more than 150 years, it's clear that Levi Strauss & Co.'s blue jeans are here to stay.

TIMELINE

xxx   xxx

1829

Loeb Strauss is born in Buttenheim, Germany, on February 26.

1846

Strauss and his family move to the United States.

1848

Gold is discovered at Sutter's Mill in California. The Gold Rush begins.

1853

Strauss arrives in San Francisco, California, on March 14. He starts a supply house called Levi Strauss.

1863

Strass renames his company Levi Strauss & Co.

1872

Jacob Davis asks Strauss to partner with him on a new type of riveted pants.

1873

Strauss and Davis's patent for the copper rivets is approved on May 20.

1886

Levi Strauss & Co. adds a leather patch to its pants.

1890

Levi Strauss & Co. changes the name of its popular XX pants to 501 jeans.

1902

Strauss dies on September 26.

1934

Levi's starts manufacturing jeans for women.

1965

Levi Strauss & Co. sets up divisions in Europe and Asia.

GLOSSARY

culture—the customs, arts, and tools of a nation or a people at a certain time.

denim—a type of cotton fabric woven with a pattern of diagonal ribs and lines.

discrimination—unfair treatment, often based on race, religion, or gender.

efficient—able to produce a desired result, especially without wasting time or energy.

incorporate—to form into a legal corporation.

incredible—extraordinary or unbelievable.

intriguing—interesting or fascinating.

Judaism—a common religion that stresses belief in one God and faithfulness to the laws of the Old Testament. People who practice this religion are Jewish.

kilt—a knee-length skirt worn by men, especially in Scotland.

lot number—an identification number assigned to a specific product during manufacturing.

mainstream—the ideas, attitudes, activities or trends that are regarded as normal or dominant in society.

marketable—fit to be offered for sale.

Middle Ages—a period in European history that lasted from about 500 CE to about 1500 CE.

philanthropist—a person who shows a spirit of goodwill toward all people, especially through generosity and charity.

rivet—a metal bolt used to fasten or secure two pieces in place.

seamstress—a woman who is skilled at sewing.

supply house—a place where merchants can go to purchase the materials they need for their businesses.

tuberculosis—a disease that affects the lungs.

tunic—a knee-length garment worn belted at the waist.

utility—usefulness.

versatile—able to do many different things well.

WEBSITES

To learn more about First in Fashion, visit **abdobooklinks.com**. These links are routinely monitored and updated to provide the most current information available.

INDEX

GUS,
the Pilgrim Turkey

Written by

Teresa Bateman

Illustrated by

Ellen Joy Sasaki

Albert Whitman & Company, Morton Grove, Illinois

Dedicated to Miss Sanford's Fourth Grade Class
at Brigadoon Elementary School 2006-2007.
Talking to you about writing your stories gave me the idea for Gus—T.B.

For Anna Kate—E.J.S.

Library of Congress Cataloging-in-Publication Data

Bateman, Teresa.
Gus, the pilgrim turkey / by Teresa Bateman ; illustrated by Ellen Joy Sasaki.
p. cm.
Summary: Gus the turkey has loved growing up on a farm, but when the other animals tell him he will soon
become Thanksgiving dinner, he decides to go south to find a place of safety.
ISBN 978-0-8075-1266-1
[1. Turkeys—Fiction. 2. Thanksgiving Day—Fiction. 3. Voyages and travels—Fiction. 4. Costume—Fiction.
5. Penguins—Fiction.] I. Sasaki, Ellen Joy, ill. II. Title.
PZ7.B294435Gus 2008 [E]—dc22 2008000053

Text copyright © 2008 by Teresa Bateman.
Illustrations copyright © 2008 by Ellen Joy Sasaki.
Published in 2008 by Albert Whitman & Company, 6340 Oakton Street, Morton Grove, Illinois 60053-2723.
Published simultaneously in Canada by Fitzhenry & Whiteside, Markham, Ontario.
Printed in China through B & P International Ltd.

10 9 8 7 6 5 4 3 2 1

The design is by Carol Gildar.

The illustrations were done in watercolor, colored pencils, and pen and ink.

For more information about Albert Whitman,
please visit our web site at www.albertwhitman.com.

Gus loved being a turkey. He gobbled with friends, got to wear whatever he pleased, and was fed almost every time he turned around. Life was fabulous.

He was young, so every day was a new adventure. In the spring, there were tasty young bugs everywhere. Gus looked stunning in his Easter hat.

Summer was even better. He danced in the sprinkler wearing shorts with crazy patterns, and he loved the way the sun glinted off the farm pond.

Now it was autumn. Gus wrapped a jaunty orange scarf around his neck.

"I can't wait for winter!" he gobbled to his friends. "I want to make snow turkeys and wear my new wooly cap. I've even bought a tuxedo for New Year's Eve!"

"I wouldn't worry about New Year's," said the horse.

"No," barked the dog. "Turkeys don't make it to January around here."

"Why not?" Gus asked.

"Thanksgiving. That's why not," the goose explained.
Gus was puzzled. So his friends told him about the
Pilgrims traveling the wild seas by ship, looking for a safe
place to live. No problem. They told him about Native
Americans who helped the Pilgrims. No problem.

They told him about the big feast. No problem.

"I LOVE food," Gus reminded them. "So, what's on the menu?" His friends told him.

BIG PROBLEM.

"NO WAY!" Gus shouted.

"It's true," said the rooster.

"Well, I'll leave. I'll just pack up and leave," Gus said.

"And go where?" the horse asked.

Gus looked up. A "V" of birds was flying by.
"South," he declared. "Other birds go south for the
winter. Maybe that's why they don't end up as dinner!"

His friends weren't sure about his plan, but they helped Gus fill his backpack with seed corn and his favorite outfits.

"Good luck!" they shouted as he gobbled out of sight.

Poor Gus's drumsticks got rather tired, but he kept walking. After several weeks he saw decorations—Pilgrims, pumpkins, and TURKEYS.

South. He knew he had to go farther south.

When Gus crossed the Rio Grande into Mexico, he felt safer. They didn't have Thanksgiving in Mexico, did they?

Gus came to a town and heard music playing nearby. He followed the happy sound to a party. Cake was on the table. Hanging from a tree was a large colorful bird. A turkey?

He couldn't tell because it wouldn't stay still. The children were beating it with a stick!

The horror, the horror!

Suddenly the bird broke. A cascade of candy fell out. Gus gasped in relief. It wasn't a turkey—it wasn't even a real bird! Still, he couldn't stay in a place where people would whack any kind of bird, feathered or fake.

Gus kept moving. Thanksgiving or not, everywhere
he went people looked at him with hungry eyes.
Was there no safe place for a turkey?
At last he grew so tired he couldn't walk anymore.

So Gus found a ship heading south and
tiptoed on board late one night.

He hopped into a lifeboat and settled
down for a long journey.

He was safe. Whew! For the first few days
he enjoyed sailing.

But soon the seas grew rough and it got cold, and then colder, and then the coldest Gus had ever felt. He tugged on his warm wooly hat.

Then one day the ship stopped. Gus poked his head out. The coast was clear! He ran to the rail and looked around. SNOW! SNOW! And more SNOW!

The ship was surrounded by snow and ice.

Gus gobbled in astonishment. Unfortunately, someone heard him.

"Hey, would you get a load of that!" said a man in a parka. "I can't believe it! It's Thanksgiving, and right on board we have a real live turkey—just in time for our Thanksgiving feast!"

Gus grabbed his backpack and charged down the gangplank. But where could he hide? In this white wilderness he stood out like a sore thumb.

Suddenly he saw a whole bunch of other birds! He dove into them. "Excuse me. Let me by. So sorry . . . "

Still, he didn't feel safe. All the others were wearing black and white. He needed a way to blend in.

Quickly Gus pulled out his tuxedo and threw it on.
There was a lot of shouting, but now the men couldn't
see Gus. Finally they headed back to the ship.

"What was that about?" the other birds asked,
"and who are you?"

"I'm Gus," Gus explained. "And I've traveled for a long, long time trying to find a place where I can be safe."

"Is a killer whale after you?" asked the nearest penguin.

"No, no," Gus replied. "It's nothing like that. It's . . . well, it's Thanksgiving."

"Thanksgiving?" chorused the penguins.

"Sure. It's a holiday about Pilgrims and stuff," Gus said.

"Penguins?" they asked.

"No, PILGRIMS," Gus said slowly. Then he explained.

The penguins listened. "So the Pilgrims left their homes because they didn't feel safe there, and they traveled by ship for a long, long time?" said the penguin leader.

Gus nodded. All the penguins turned to eye the nearby ship.

"Welcome, Pilgrim!" the head penguin announced.

"But I'm not a . . . " Gus began, and then he looked at the natives in his strange new home. They looked like they'd help him survive.

"Maybe I AM a Pilgrim," Gus said at last. "I sure have a lot to be thankful for."

"Then how about a feast?" asked his new friends.

Gus grinned. "NO PROBLEM!"